C000096546

Good News for a Postmodern World

Colin Horseman

Priest-in-Charge, Great Horkesley

GROVE BOOKS LIMITED

RIDLEY HALL RD CAMBRIDGE CB3 9HU

Contents

The Cover Illustration is by Penny Horseman

Copyright Colin Horseman 1996

First Impression August 1996
Second Impression March 1999
ISSN 0953-4946
ISBN 1 85174 323 5

1

The Present Scene

Those who recall 'Tom & Jerry' cartoons will remember how the plot altered little. The mouse would suffer a variety of attacks from the cat, find himself cornered, narrowly avoid annihilation and then, by a neat combination of luck and cheeky courage, come out on top in the final frame. Church historians will find a familiar ring about part of that scenario at least, when they think of the recent history of the Western church.

Are You a Church or a Mouse?

At the dawn of the Reformation the medieval church had been mighty but had become overweight, unfit and increasingly ineffective. It had held sway over a culture that had largely shared its worldview and values, and had received its ministrations gladly. This was a unified field of belief and values where heaven, hell and all spiritual things were as unquestionably real and present as the material world. Thomas Aquinas, the great philosopher-theologian of the Middle Ages, had made a masterly synthesis of faith and reason in his great *Summa Theologica*. This had become the text book of ideology for the time. Truth was found in the teaching of the church, derived from a received interpretation of the Scriptures, informed by sometimes obscure philosophical reasoning. 'Truth' was given and received, not sought after by observation or experiment. Concepts like 'scientific verification' or 'experiment' were either unknown or denounced as heresy.

The Reformation was a spiritual revival and a revolution in many ways. But it did not challenge the presupposition that truth was a 'given,' and that any coherent world view could only begin from revelation about God, his nature and purpose of salvation. But the Reformation went hand-in-hand with a new burst of intellectual and technological invention. The church, accustomed to more stately movement, suddenly found itself being chased by a developing, newly confident Renaissance movement. The Ptolemaic view of the universe and archaic philosophical premises which had been the feet on which it stood, were being knocked away.

From then on, things moved rather quickly in historical terms. Chased by the Renaissance the church soon found itself coming under vicious attack from human reason, which achieved almost divine status in the eighteenth century. Reeling from the blows, the church backed into the technological and sociological upheavals of the nineteenth century dazed and disoriented, with nowhere to hide. Running into the twentieth century it found itself battered again by 'modernism' in the growing belief that science and science alone can provide the truth. 'If you cannot prove it scientifically it cannot be true.' God, the world of the spiritual, heaven and hell, became at best subjective categories to be used if absolutely necessary, and at worst outmoded presuppositions worthless because 'unscientific.'

Dodging these blows it almost tripped up over an accompanying despair and disillusionment which followed on two world wars and was expressed by various forms of existentialist philosophy.[1]

Existentialism affected much popular culture in the sixties. The writings of Jean-Paul Sartre, the plays of Camus and the thinking of Carl Jaspers found their way into a generation of pop music, protest and permissiveness. At its heart existentialism was a search for the meaning of personhood. Such meaning was not to be found in systems of truth and external, imposed standards, but by the way in which we authenticate ourselves. How we choose became less significant than the fact that we do choose. Choice, decision, actions and interaction became the hallmarks of human existence. This was one of the cross-rhythms to which the sixties was swinging. Some of the most influential existentialists (such as Sartre) were atheists. Most of them, even existentialist theologians, abandoned traditional ideas of revelation and religion. By and large the church failed to develop an adequate response to the challenges these thinkers were presenting.

Many impartial observers believe that the *coup de grâce* is about to be delivered to the church by the prevailing climate of thought and belief which has come to be known as 'postmodernism.'[2]

A Mood and Impatience

Postmodernism is not a self-contained, coherent philosophy. In fact it is not a philosophy at all. It is better understood as being the mood of the nineties, expressed in various forms. As a reaction against the analytical, rigid, rational approach of modernism we see an increasing impatience with absolute values. This applies to ethics and morals. Leading a fifth-form tutorial in an inner city comprehensive school I struggled to get the students to find any abiding principles which they could apply to personal relationships. A conversation with the tutor afterwards revealed a deep suspicion in her that I was trying to impose external values. For her the objective was to help them to think out a personal approach for themselves; what it was did not matter.

The postmodern impatience goes deeper, and touches on the concept of truth itself. Truth is what you want it to be. Truth is 'It works for me. OK?' Postmodern thinkers have fostered a deep distrust of 'meta-narratives.' By that is meant the versions of history or truth which have been developed over the years by people in power, in order to maintain the *status quo* and their own élite position within it. Watch television programmes on historical subjects to see a postmodern reaction at work. It is possible to have a black version of history, a feminist version of history, a minorities version of history with no search for objectivity in the frame at all.

---

1   G E Veith, *Guide to Contemporary Culture* (Crossway, 1994), pp 35f; Board of Mission, *Good News In Our Times—The Gospel and Contemporary Cultures* (Church House Publishing, 1991) pp 14f.

2   See I Cundy (ed), *Tomorrow's Another Country: Education in a Postmodern World* (General Synod Board of Education, 1996) and Veith, *ibid.*

Over the centuries Christian 'meta-narratives' have inspired the Crusades, justified slavery and theories of racial supremacy, and linked mission with imperial expansion. If we want to proclaim the gospel with integrity we need to own up to these things. We need to recognize the validity of postmodern comment and we need to think carefully and honestly about the myths and misunderstandings which might be compromising the gospel even today. What are the 'meta-narratives' which stand in the way of our evangelism?

Such a question must prompt us to look again at the form and content of our proclamation. How do we present the moral challenge of the gospel? People living together outside of wedlock might easily feel that they are being forced into a manipulative value system if they are dealt with unsympathetically when they approach the church for marriage or baptism. If someone responds to the gospel should their way of life be regularized before they are given church membership? Is acceptance of the moral imperative a condition of receiving the gospel, or a consequence? In this same context we need to re-examine our use of apologetic in evangelism. It is no longer adequate to state simply that Christianity helps us to keep the standards we know are right. We often need to begin further back than that. We need to be prepared to argue that there are standards given by God and, because of who he is and the quality of his love, those standards are not repressive and negative but lead to the fullness of life.

Postmodern Belief

At the same time postmodernists would want to affirm the value of spirituality. Our contemporary culture is anything but secular, even though one still hears Christian spokespeople making that assertion. Secularism went out with scientific modernism. The difference between this non-Christian understanding and a Christian approach is the belief that no one spirituality has an exclusive claim to be the truth. Jesus, his example and his message can stand alongside other spiritual sources as one option, on a 'pic-'n'-mix' basis. Joanna Lumley, writing in *Woman's Weekly* in 1990, looked forward to a more spiritual approach in the nineteen nineties. In the same year a Gallup poll of eleven- to sixteen-year-olds found that fifty-nine per cent believed in God. The *X Files* cult television series has as its sub-theme the belief that aliens are real in their effect on the human spirit. This interest in spirituality comes out in survey after survey when people express their openness to Jesus alongside their rejection of the church.[3]

There is much about postmodernism which is dangerous and destructive. But there are aspects which are attractive and positive, and which redress the balance of dry, scientific rationalism. Playfulness, an openness to the supernatural, a valuing of the environment, all are characteristics with which we can sympathize. In responding to the playful, the importance of 'game' and fun, we need to look again at the possibilities for spontaneity in our presentation of the gospel. John Drane has presented a persuasive picture of how evangelism can and should

---

3   See Graham Cray. *From Here To Where?* (Board of Mission Occasional Paper number 3).

happen in worship. But for that to take place there has to be a reflection in that worship of the openness and freedom which is a fact of life for many people. The use of quick-fire drama, silences and visual images can be of real value in opening people to the gospel and in communicating something of its impact. However, such tools need to be used both appropriately and well. For all its playfulness and whimsicality the postmodern age is used to good professional presentation.

In terms of the environment it is perhaps astonishing that the church is often seen as a villain in the piece, given that the God whom we worship is the Creator, that his Son is the agent of creation, and that his Spirit is pledged to uphold and develop the creation and our place in it. Generations of Christians have received a version of the gospel which is shaped by individualism and a pre-occupation with the 'spiritual,' leading us to neglect or even transgress the mandate God has given us to respect and manage sympathetically the world he has given us. A postmodern generation challenges us in this area to develop an approach and an apologetic which is more in line with God's whole counsel. This is true in spite of the more extreme aspects of environmental thinking which deify the earth, and dehumanize humanity.

So, in the face of the postmodern culture the question remains. Will the church escape? Is there some act of bravado we can perform to avoid yet another staggering blow? Will the church-mouse escape the culture-cat and be able to bolt home to safety?

On This Rock

It is more than time to change the metaphor. The purpose of this book is to look at the culture and worldviews we in Britain are heir to: to discover how, as the church of Christ, we fulfil our calling to share the good news of Christ in ways which address, redeem and transform society. If, as Christ promised, even the gates of hell cannot prevail against his church, then we can expect doors to open as we follow him in obedience.

The historical sketch given above is a helicopter view of history, much obscured by cloud, missing out some important features of the landscape, necessarily deficient in detail. But several important factors emerge—important for us if we are to share good news with postmodern Britain.

First, culture is not tidy in its development. Loose ends from one prevailing worldview trail out and weave themselves into the next. Paradigm shifts mix up the various strata of ideas into a conglomerate of philosophies. So, in our country today we find all the views sketched out above. At a recent clergy training day I invited participants to comment on how they saw their communities affected by the philosophies we were reviewing. One parish priest said with great conviction, 'In my village most people would certainly hold a medieval view of faith'! So also in postmodernist Britain we can expect to engage with people who, in the best modernist tradition, want proof before they can believe. Doubt about the miracles of the Bible will sometimes appear in the same conversation as an account of a psychic experience or a devoutly expressed view that a loved one is in heaven. People desperate to believe in God will need to view him/her/it as an Alien. Someone with a vigorous integrity in academic terms will practise the most developed relativism in personal relationships and morals.

Second, this developmental complexity is overlaid by global factors. The geographical limitations of our medieval forbears have dissolved as surely as their intellectual ones. Young and not-so-young people are searching for religious satisfaction not only in the classic religions of the East and West, but in the exciting, throbbing religious climate of Africa and Native North America.

Third—and the previous paragraph leads us into this—our culture has no one clear feature or characteristic, perhaps more than any which preceded it. It is a 'pic-'n'-mix' culture in terms of its religion, entertainment and philosophy. It is rare to find a convert to Buddhism, or to one of the tribal religions of Africa or North America. But people will form their own views with bits of each. Articles in teen magazines do not display coherent existentialism, or materialism, or any other '-ism.' Features from everywhere blend in a mixture which does, it has to be said, sometimes seem rather glorious!

Fourth, all of this is set against a doomsday backdrop. The close of the millennium aside, nuclear holocaust fears have given way to environmental concerns in raising for many people big questions about the survival of the planet. We live with two opposing reactions to this: hedonism; and the development of new absolutes. The designer-drug user will insist on ozone-friendly deodorant to use before going out to the rave!

Before we move on to look more closely at the influence of these cultural developments in society, some lessons are already emerging for a church which wants to be real with the gospel in this kind of world. That we have an image problem cannot be doubted. But the biggest problem is that the perceived image of the remote, naive, bumbling but well-meaning religious practitioner can be uncomfortably close to the truth! What we have already seen about our contemporary culture should teach us three things:

a) That we should study and study carefully the religious quest of our contemporaries.[4] Some evangelism training packages have emphasized the importance of learning a systematic and often quite substantial version of the gospel.[5] The aim has then been to make a presentation of this version of the gospel. Such an approach has been, and in some contexts still could be, highly effective. But really, today is not a day for the packaged presentation. We need to be more about hearing the questions people are asking, anticipating the gaps in their home-made spiritual understanding, and being ready to give pointers to the true and living way. Such 'evangelism on the wing' may sometimes seem to be a chancy fragmented business. But behind it all is a God who cares for the lost and who works through the variety and availability of his people. We

---

4   On this see P Sampson, V Samuel, C Sugden (ed), *Faith and Modernity* (Regnum Lynx, 1994).
5   For instance, Evangelism Explosion. Breakthrough.

still need to grow into a deep understanding of our faith. But we need to be ready to be used as part of a wider picture, links in a chain or pieces in jigsaw of a person's spiritual quest.[6]

b) That we should seek ways to present the uniqueness of our faith as a dynamic reality. Neither assimilation into the melting pot nor defensive attempts at preservation are appropriate. What will make an impact on a deprived, inner city community is not a paternalistic, patronizing concern for the poor, seeking to give them a way to become middle-class like normal Christians. Rather it will be a gospel which leads to a true recognition and valuing of people in the love of God, a developing of gifts which are appropriate to the situation and a serious attempt to work out the redeeming and renewing love of God and the issues which concern, oppress and incapacitate people. In another community, a decision made about a career move on ethical and Christian grounds rather than a materialistic and selfish one, could say much to neighbours, family and colleagues about the way our faith works.

c) That as a matter of urgent policy, those with recognized gifts in the area of cultural sensitivity and innovative ministry should be commissioned to increase awareness in the church, and should develop an effective apologetic.

To these issues we shall return later.

2

Critical Paths

It is often held that movements, like 'Modernism,' 'Postmodernism,' 'Existentialism' and so on, are confined to the rarefied circles of academic debate, moving from one professor's study to another's lecture theatre, touching ground nowhere in between and finally disappearing like a cloud of senior common room cigar smoke. Those who hold this view say that we need to get on with the real job of evangelism, dealing with people in the real world and leave the other issues to the university chaplains!

Nothing could be further from the truth. In the present chapter I want to show how these paradigm shifts in philosophy and culture affect people inside and outside the churches, via the media, politics and the economy and education.

The Media

Clearly the pervasive presence of the media is one of the most significant changes to have happened within living memory. It follows that media people

---

6 Again, see Sampson, Samuel and Sugden, *op cit.*

have become some of the most significant people in the lives of most of us. News editors and presenters determining what we see and do not see of world affairs, helping us to form opinions. Documentary makers presenting information, introducing us to new ways of thinking. Entertainers make us laugh. The storytellers common to all cultures have a vital role in forming opinion presenting and preserving values, giving and expressing a common mind. For us they are the scriptwriters and producers of the soaps and sitcoms.[6]

This is not the protective 'Auntie' of affectionate remembrance, nor the 'Big Brother' who dominated Winston Smith.[8] Rather it is a collection of highly professional, highly-trained, highly-motivated individuals, fallible and impressionable like the rest of us, and like the rest of us open to the influence of what they see and hear. This is how ideologies and worldviews spread. The student of yesterday is the media-person of today. What was the stuff of a lecture yesterday is a play, comedy routine or arts programme this evening. These are the 'critical paths' along which opinion runs.

The highly developed nature of media skills and technology has combined with other factors and means that an increasing number of people are 'non-book' people. And this is true through all social groupings. This is not to say that people do not read books; what has changed is the place now given to the written word in the forming of culture. The burgeoning publishing industry deals mostly with entertainment, leisure and practical issues, over against the dissemination and discussion of ideas. Even those books which do handle philosophical issues do so on a 'key to successful living' basis. Ideas, opinions and worldviews come, even for thinking people, as 'preformed' packages, enabling us to take up instant attitudes to the issues facing us.

Truth and Practice

This has several implications for society in general and for the Christian faith in particular. First it colours our understanding of truth. 'It works therefore it will do' as an opinion, a solution, a value. Without the tradition of history and careful thought represented by the world of books, truth becomes a pragmatic, relative business. Clearly this is an issue for a faith heavily dependent on 'the Word of God' whose historic frame of reference is the Bible (literally 'Book'), and which proclaims a belief in absolute values.

In actual fact, at this point our culture is challenging us to rediscover the real nature of biblical revelation. Essentially the Bible is not meant to be a static, written record of what God did once. The Old Testament and New Testament in different ways present the Word of God as being dynamic and active, presenting its impact in many different forms. Sometimes it is dramatic; sometimes poetic; it uses history, imagination, reflection; story, song and celebration. Evangelism today needs to find ways to let the Bible be all of this. Imaginative presentation of

---

7 As this booklet was being written *Eastenders* featured a girl's conversion to Christianity and the issues that raised in her family. A useful resource for churches to study?
8 See George Orwell, *1984.*

the message needs study of the Bible which lets it come in to where people are in their experience and questioning. Drama, use of videos and computer software packages are all practical ways in which the gospel can speak today.[9] Go into any major tourist town on a fine day in summer and somewhere a crowd will have gathered round street entertainers. Jugglers, uni-cyclists and fire eaters have fun and others share it. Can it be beyond the wit and imagination of Christians to find similar expertise amongst us to be used to draw a crowd and point to Jesus?[10] Our first inroad with the gospel is not reasoned presentation but impact. Jesus came to give life, not logic, in all its fullness.

Second, there is an issue about personhood. On the one hand there seems to be an increasing individualism. It is possible to view the world, review ideas and opinions and make connections of thought and information without leaving the isolation of one's own room. On the other hand this very isolation leaves us open to manipulation by, or at least to influence from, a very few opinion-formers. Viewing, as opposed to reading or discussion, is a passive activity. We become dependent for our opinions on what we are told we ought to be thinking. Combine this with a decreasing sense of history and the rejection of existing absolutes and the scene is set for a clear loss of personhood in terms of our opinions and decisions. If Christians can let their minds be renewed by the Spirit of God then they make a valuable contribution to the question for meaning and personhood. But in our postmodern world this will not be done by writing worthy books or uttering wordy pronouncements. It will be done in the more messy and more costly business of involvement with people for their sake, because we love them. I recently visited a group of non-Christian people living on an isolated farm— escapees from modernist, materialist world. Their home has become an unofficial refuge for women at risk. They care about people; their concern became known and people were attracted. They have no message to proclaim, no self-assured answers to give; but their love itself is a message. The children of this generation are often wiser indeed than the children of light.

Reality and Perception

Along with these issues of truth and personhood, comes a third, related factor to do with reality, or our perception of it. What do we know about the real international and global issues? Can we only ever know what others choose to tell us? On a more local level, virtual reality entertainment and immediate access to our imagination and dreams makes us vulnerable and, in some cases, unclear about what is real and what is not.

In the midst of these confusions it needs to be remembered that, in spite of the postmodernist credo, there are absolute values being canvassed—the view that there are no absolutes is an absolute view! In seeking to share the good news we

---

9 For instance 'Jesus Then And Now' also the 'Jesus Video Project.' c/o Agape, Fairgate House, Kings Road, Tyseley, Birmingham B11 2AA

10 Christian clowning has had a vogue but perhaps has not been fully exploited evangelistically by the church at large.

would do well to give some thought to what the new absolutes are, and who are their proponents. This would help us to focus our apologetic and be clear about the language and concepts we want to use.

Politics and the Economy[11]

On the surface, affairs of state might seem to be aloof from the postmodernist playfulness of the media world. But the same presuppositions are at work here also. It is true that politics has always been 'the art of the possible' to a large extent, but that pragmatism has usually been informed by an agreed code of conduct. It has been focused on a 'moral consensus' even with all the attendant hypocrisy and posturing we know so well. Our present age has brought with it an almost total disillusionment with party politics as we know it. As a result those seeking power or seeking to retain power become more and more governed by a consumer-driven agenda. This moves them away from absolutes to programmes designed to appeal to the perceived wants of the electoral market. Sadly for the politicians this has served only to increase the sense of disillusionment.

There are matters which feel important to people, but they are usually in areas where normal politics cannot move freely, because of compromise with conflicting interests. So concern over environmental matters, homelessness and injustice become 'issue politics,' increasingly drawing people together from wide age and social ranges. But such politics do not have and do not seek to have long-term coherence or identity. They speak of the fragmentation of our society and our prevailing tendency to live for now. History is dead and the future may never happen.

In the world of the economy there has been disillusionment too. The boom-utopia went bust. The welfare state is being eroded; a sound manufacturing base has given way to leisure and service based growth. Short-termism and self-preservation have become the economic order of the day. Increased overall wealth seems inconsistent with a perceived individual need for more. There has recently been published a handbook for job success in what it calls the 'Information Age.'[12] Coincidentally it is an excellent example of how to communicate an important message! Among its headlines we find advice like: 'Become a quick-change artist'; 'Mobility, not mourning (for what once was) makes you a valuable member of the group'; 'Speed up'; 'Accept ambiguity and uncertainty'; 'See yourself as a service centre'; 'Manage your own morale'; 'Alter your expectations.' Important spiritual dynamics are at work here which we miss to our cost. Can we free the Christian message from the materialism which wound itself round it in a previous generation? Can we engage meaningfully with the readers of that handbook to say that in the midst of uncertainty, risk and change there is a living God who will go with you and guide you?

---

11 M Eden (ed), *Britain On The Brink* (Crossway, 1993), pp 44f; see also D E Jenkins, *God, Politics and the Future* (SCM, 1988).

12 See P Pritchett, *New Work Habits For a Radically Changing World* (Pritchett Associates, 1994).

Ironically, it is the many young people with 'alternative' lifestyles who currently live a protest against arid materialism. Yet they are caught in the contradictions. Their protest is funded by the contributions of those who do serve mammon. Christianity, the professed enemy of materialism, fares no better.

Transatlantic Christianity has become a laughing-stock because of its compromise with wealth. An exercise I often do with people is to write the word 'evangelism' on a chart and ask for the words which immediately come to mind. On more than one occasion the words 'money' or 'financial exploitation' have been offered! Our English Christianity, whilst not tarred with the same brush, does sometimes look a little like the religious end of a consumer spectrum. A return to a full biblical integrity about the possession and stewardship of money could light a path through current confusion.[13] The dominant work ethic so often used to oppress the poor and create an elite is not the only alternative. In the meantime ambivalence about economic matters is bound to stay. 'Hate the rich but love the riches' will be the watchword of a culture where an envied few make the millions, but millions buy the lottery ticket which will open up opportunity for them.

Education[14]

Preoccupation with education has dominated the thinking of all political parties. That signals to us that it is an issue which affects the hearts and lives of all people, directly and indirectly. Parents often sense there has been a sea-change both in terms of what is taught and in the way in which teaching takes place. And they are right. Theories of education which guide what happens in classrooms reflect some of the postmodernist principles we described earlier. The emphasis is upon equipping students to judge for themselves the implications of a historical or ethical or personal situation, rather than absorbing information as 'given.' The existing 'meta-narratives' are to be challenged and not simply accepted as fact. The voice and experience of the oppressed must be sought and heard. On the face of it this is a healthy option. In practice it can become the substituting of one ideology for another. Debates over the teaching of religion in schools have often missed the point. The issue is not about whether Christianity remains our national religion and should therefore be taught. It is rather about whether in principle, an absolutist approach should be adopted. Pluralism and relativism in moral education have become the new absolutes.

Even in the teaching of science there is increasing relativism and uncertainty. The developing insights into the 'chaos principle' mean that there has to be less certainty, less emphasis on unquestioned givens than previously. Nothing can be known absolutely. Along with the existentialist approach of many in education, the scene is set for the principles and presuppositions we talked of earlier to enter the minds, hearts and homes of many who pass through the education system.

I have tried, in the above review, to indicate the way in which the ideas current

---

13 See Grove Spirituality booklet 58 *Why Be Generous?* by Roland Riem.
14 On this see Cundy, *op cit.*

in our culture are widespread in their influence and effects. The implications of this for the church are profound. Given the marked shift away from absolute values, even truth itself as a viable concept, the church and its leaders often feel marginalized. One way to escape from that is to become increasingly insular. My wife recently helped in a parish mission. In a preparation meeting she suggested to a group of church people that they should pray for one or two of their non-Christian friends whom they might invite to various events. One person, in genuine distress, said 'But I try to make sure all my friendships are among church people!' One clergyman, in a discussion on postmodernism, simply said, 'I am too involved in the life of my church to have time to think of all that!'

This insularity can show itself in the expectations of congregations. Church is sometimes seen as a refuge from an uncertain world, a bastion in which the old values can be safely defended. That is a partial truth. But the other half of the equation is that the church is meant to be a steward of the good news, a channel to communicate God's love, a bridge over which the traffic of his presence can flow. What lessons do we need to learn?

3

Lessons to Learn

In the face of the postmodern culture around us it is easy to become defensive. Sometimes the moral stance of Christians can seem like that. It is equally easy to become uncritical and accommodating. Wanting to be tolerant we become unclear. How do we free ourselves from the horns of this dilemma?

We Need to Listen

As has been shown, people in today's world live with a vast range of ideas and presuppositions. It is not possible today (if indeed it ever was) to prejudge what a person might be thinking. If we are to engage in conversation, we need to hear what people say, with a background knowledge which can help us to understand the significance of their thinking. But the precondition of listening is meeting. There is the insularity mentioned above; there is also what Vincent Donovan calls the 'Choke-law.'[15] This is the principle which absorbs time and spiritual energy upon pastoral and maintenance matters which should properly be spent in engaging with those outside the church. Both of these mean that a conscious effort should properly be spent in engaging with those outside the church—in creating real 'meeting' with people, as opposed to 'meetings' which are internal and

---

15 V E Donovan. *Christianity Rediscovered* (SCM. 1982) p 99.

business-oriented.

For some church members this may mean a conscious decision to join a group in the community rather than agreeing to be on yet another church committee. Does being 'salt and light' really mean another evening a week in the church hall discussing outreach, or does it mean going to the community association or carnival committee, where friendships can be formed, conversations struck up, decisions influenced? For others, being 'salt and light' means resisting the pressure to join all the activities necessary to keep the ecclesiastical show on the road. Instead they will take time to meet neighbours and work associates socially, go on outings with them, have a drink with them, and not feel guilty about it!

For some churches this has meant a conscious change to the programme of the church. Members are encouraged to limit their activity to one 'taking in' and one 'giving out' per week, others arrange all church meetings for one night. For others it means a radical change to the way in which non-Christians are engaged. One incumbent arranges a series of discussion evenings in someone's home, to which anyone is invited. He (or another church member) spends five minutes explaining why he is a Christian, then invites others to explain why they are not. The ensuing discussion is an opportunity to listen and to learn.

Of course such developments mean that for many churches there would have to be a great deal of change. Some groups would cease to function altogether. Some activities would come to an end because no-one would be there to keep them going. Looking at the programme in this way would make us apply different criteria to our church life. We would no longer be looking round to see who could operate the structures and maintain the status quo. We would be looking instead at our missionary call and we would be saying 'How do we best respond to that?' Our criteria of success would be restated. No longer would it be 'How busy are we?' Rather it would be 'How effective are we at making disciples?' Church growth would be radically redefined. Often we are desperate to increase the membership roll by whatever means, in order to fill the rotas or pay the quotas. If it is transfer growth or illusory growth we do not mind too much because it keeps us in *moto perpetuo*. But the changes outlined above would focus our thinking on growth as the making of new disciples, and the quality development of their discipleship. Then there would be much rejoicing in heaven!

We Need to Learn

Many Christian leaders and many church members have led sheltered lives. That is true at least in terms of spiritual quest. Born into a Christian household, or converted when the non-Christian world was a very different place, it is easy simply not to know of the pressures, influences and experiences of those around us. We need to learn, by listening, reading, thinking and debating, about the culture in which we live. If you like, this is our equivalent of Paul's tour around the Athenian pantheon (Acts 17.16f).

But in listening and responding to those outside the church we can also learn about the breakdowns in our own understanding. It is a singular fact that the views and presuppositions of those outside the church often develop as a reaction to things the church got wrong, or to gaps in our presentation of the good news. Have we always got it right about how we relate to God's creation? Have we not confused worldly power with spiritual power and seen the church in the business of manipulation and domination? Has not the uniqueness of Christianity sometimes been misrepresented as the exclusiveness of our ideas about Christianity? Humility and openness can take us a long way down the road to greater understanding.

We Need to be Resourced

What we have said so far relates to the local level. On a national level we have many fine thinkers and experienced church leaders of spiritual maturity. It would be a positive move to explore ways in which these people could come together, on an occasional but formal basis, to form a resource for the wider church. 'Change is here to stay!' Those training for ministry, those in leadership already, those called to minister in their daily work and life, could be helped enormously by such a 'think-tank.' On the one hand, ongoing research into ideas and philosophical developments could be conducted. On the other hand guidance for the churches in new forms of ministry could be applied at local level. When the church's finances suffered there was an immediate response. The expertise was already around but it was focused rapidly, and directed effectively at the problem. Our need to make up the deficit in communication with our culture is no less urgent.

Nor would such a resource group need merely to be reactive. Today's mission shows us the ongoing need for a developed and developing apologetic. Popular writers on science, ethics, morals, (the problem page gurus) on personal development, treat Christianity not as an enemy but as an irrelevance. Many false assumptions about Christian belief and practice go unchallenged. The need for a wise, far-reaching and effective apologetic is fundamental. It would be profitable to see how such a resource group could be established, maintained and used effectively to help and encourage the wider church, as well as to address issues at a national level.

We Need a Real Spirituality

There is a confusion over what is reality and what is not. Abstract concepts of truth cause problems. But there is a clear search for something that works, that makes a difference. And there is a persistent, nagging, spiritual hunger. Someone who responded to an invitation to an *Alpha* group, and who subsequently became a Christian, responded in the first instance because of the quality and integrity of the person who invited her. Initially it was not about claims of truth or a moral challenge. That did indeed come later, but what mattered at first was seeing a person whose life was different. If we live in a spiritually hungry culture, have we ourselves found the food that truly satisfies? Do we offer that real food in the Spirit of Jesus? Integrity and reality do matter.

This integrity and reality does not only relate to the way in which we live out our faith. It also lies at the heart of our understanding of our faith. Even though many Christians do not consciously adopt the ideas of contemporary culture, there is always a process of osmosis, by which attitudes and opinions are unconsciously taken in and put into practice. In a consumer-led world it is easy to let our spirituality be determined by what seems to give instant satisfaction to surface needs. Of course the quest for purity of intention and expression in religion can never be successful. But the search for integrity means that we can not afford to ignore the difficult issues of discipleship which Jesus lays before us—sacrifice, commitment, accepting his truth even when it hurts. Only as we deepen our relationship with him in and through these, will we present a faith worth looking at for our contemporaries.

In order to follow that through we need to look now at the gospel we share, and how we share it, with a postmodern world.

4

The Gospel We Share

In my early Christian life I was brought up to believe that everything essential to the gospel, all that the world needed to know, was present in the New Testament. I still believe that, but in a different way. I see the New Testament revelation not as a package, all the contents of which should be displayed simultaneously, to the world. Rather it is like a seed which contains the whole plant, but which unfolds different aspects at different times. And so for any age there are particular facets of gospel truth which form the 'leading edge' (to change the picture). They feed in, and the rest follows in due course.

What are those 'leading edge' aspects of the gospel for the world at the turn of the millennium?

Relationship

Both in terms of personal experience, and in more abstract philosophical terms, personal relationship is a key area of need and exploration. On the abstract level the heirs of existentialism find it difficult to present relationships as anything other than a means to gain personal satisfaction. One-sided approaches like that must self-destruct in the end. On the personal level, as one rather disillusioned road protester and commune dweller said to me recently; 'All these ideals are great till people get involved. People mess it all up!'

Rightly understood and practised with integrity Christianity first gives a reason for broken relationships, then points a way forward to their restoration. At the heart of this restoration is a renewed understanding of personhood, seeing both its worth (made in the image of God) and its failings (marred through rebellion against him). The way to renewed relationships is not only modelled by Jesus but also activated by him. His life-force gives the resources to forgive, be committed, and to love. His worldview gives us a reason for trying. Ultimately the wellspring of all of this is the three-in-one lifestyle of the Godhead—a perfect relationship where each personality is respected and honoured and finds ultimate satisfaction through the worth imparted to the other personalities. Rather than being a symbol of authoritarian domination and intellectual complexity the Trinity is seen in true biblical light; as the dynamic, authentic source of life-in-relationship as it is meant to be lived.

If that is true then we have to take relationship issues very seriously. Perhaps one of the reasons for the great success of *Alpha* groups as a means of evangelism is their opportunity to develop real friendships over a meal, and to have a suitable forum where an existing friendship can find natural expression in sharing the gospel. One church in a mining area opened up a missionary opportunity amongst men by inviting a number to help with a small building project. The environment of bricks, sand and cement was one where they felt at home and relaxed. Their skills and expertise were truly valued, and their integrity was respected. Questions about the ultimate purpose of the building were answered honestly; real friendships were formed with Christian men involved in the project and people came to faith. What setting would your church need for the forming of genuine relationships with non-Christians? Do such settings already exist? If not, could your church create such settings naturally and well?

Similarly, the earthly life and ministry of Jesus is seen as the linking and renewing of the life of God with his children. The taking on of human personhood gives a clear invitation to take personhood seriously. The death of Jesus on the cross, rather than being seen as a cold, legal transaction, is in reality an emotional, extravagant outburst of love as you have never seen it before. His rising, going to the Father and sending of the Spirit is an assurance that we are not left to thread our way alone through the labyrinth. That view of the human pilgrimage was heroic to the rationalists, absurd to the existentialists, pointless and silly to postmodernity. The revelation of God in Christ shows how it really is meant to be—God's people finding out about his world in company with him and learning to live with one another…which brings us to the church.

Community—The Church as the Body of Christ

God never intended to deal in abstractions. That is why Jesus came and that is why the church came into being. It is a deep irony that the body which was meant to be the love and truth of God in action and the means of sharing his good news, has become, in the West, the chief obstacle to all of that happening. 'Jesus—yes; the church—no!' is the resounding verdict of many people now.

We simply do not have the option to return to the private, individual pietism of an earlier age. In some ways that would suit the mood of our culture. But in so doing we would back away from the challenge and opportunity to show forth the positive side of Christian insights about belonging together. In addition we would lose sight of the fact that, like it or not, the church is part of the gospel message—not a medium for it, not ancillary to it, but part and parcel of the good news. It is part of the process by which people are initiated into the kingdom of God. So how do we build our missionary congregations for this age and the age to come?[16]

i) The Faith We Share

Traditionally the focus for Christian unity and corporate life has been the faith we hold in common. The creeds stand as a liturgical expression of this, and traditionally bishops gained their authority as guardians of orthodoxy. This is not an easy concept to live with in the postmodern world. The views of truth we discussed earlier, suspicion about the 'meta-narratives' and a new experience of pluralist society all cast an unflattering light upon propositional truth statements like the Nicene Creed, the Thirty-nine Articles, or the Westminster Confession.

There is something important for us to listen to here. The Creeds and historic formularies all came into being to deal with specific issues. They were raised out of varying cultural backgrounds, ranging from neo-Platonist to Reformation-Renaissance. Some of the apologetic material based on these formularies took on a distinctly rationalist feel. We have no mandate to perpetuate the formularies *for their own sake*. What is important is that we seek, as they did, to explore the Scriptures afresh, to discover and interpret their significance for those whom we are called to serve with the gospel. Only a fool would ignore them; but the truly wise course is not to present or re-present them as being fitting or adequate for this age and the future. Rather they can serve as one resource amongst many to help us find a creative understanding of biblical truth for today. That truth will not be static but will be such as can guide and form and reform a pilgrim church moving amongst a restless, searching generation. We owe it to the culture we serve not to have to make the issues they face fit our version of the truth. Rather, we listen to the issues, and let the biblical truth address them in dynamic, life-giving ways.

As an example of this we may look at how we view family.[17] We have inherited a way of believing that the Christian way of life is expressed in a nuclear family situation involving marriage and lifelong commitment. Faced with a breakdown of this pattern around us do we despair and become critical of a flight from Christianity, or do we recognize the complexities and try to minister into them with compassionate Christian care—not least because some of the disruption is due to the hypocrisies of an earlier age?

ii) The Life We Share

Many of the ideological and societal changes we have looked at result in an increased hunger for something that is real, a way of life that has meaning . Never

---

16 On this see R W Warren, *Building Missionary Congregations* (Church House Publishing, 1995).
17 M Eden, *op cit*, pp 55f.

was there a more urgent need to reflect the truth and power of the gospel in the life of the church. We need a new way of looking at this. Evangelism has often been seen either as a 'bolt-on-extra' or as a special and specialized activity almost opposed to the pastoral concern of the church. Perhaps we need to revisit a view of 'evangelization' which is about the life of the gospel running through all that we are and all that we do.

I knew a church where the incumbent had a great heart for evangelism. So committed and enthusiastic was he that before long he had formed a very effective team who visited in the parish, were warmly welcomed, and saw a good number of people make a positive response to the gospel. Yet the church did not grow. Why was that? Many of those who had embraced the caring presentation of the gospel found a mismatch when they visited the church. The atmosphere was not friendly; the worship was formal and clergy-dominated. There was no discernible 'gospel-dynamic' in people's responses to and relationships with one another.

On the other hand a small village church, with no discernible evangelism strategy, is making a positive impact on the people around, and a number are joining the congregation. The reason? Those village Christians take their faith seriously and work it out in all kinds of ways. Help is given to the needy and that is soon known. Visitors to the service find a warm and genuine welcome and find people they know and respect from other settings taking this gospel business seriously. So they conclude that there must be something in it.

Together with the search for reality goes the need for personhood. The New Testament concept of the body of Christ is tailor-made to meet this need. Perhaps the time has come to overhaul our church's leadership training entirely so that it focuses more and more on the gifts, grace and wisdom needed to empower this model. Personhood cannot develop in isolation despite the internet and whatever other quasi-relationship mechanisms might be developed. Personhood for creatures made in the image of God is about giving ourselves in love that serves, within a framework of love that secures. It is about finding, celebrating and offering our Godlike qualities of creativity whilst learning how to direct them to their true end.

Church leaders can often be heard bemoaning the lack of human resources in their church. 'We need more people from a professional background.' 'If people from the suburbs would move into the inner city and join our church we could really start to develop.' What an insult to the people of the community! The retired foreman or the head cleaning lady will probably have exactly the gifts of leadership their church needs. The village church, bemoaning its tiny congregation, will no doubt contain a fund of local knowledge, deep faith and perseverance which can blossom into mission. It may not be the model taught in the Bible College classroom, but it will be those people being enabled to offer themselves, as God made them, back to him. Such a respect and renewal of personhood gives a clear gospel message to the world around.

For our gospel to be credible it must be seen to produce those results. With a very few exceptions we do not even seem to be trying. Teach the teachers, train the trainees, resource the shepherds and the trickle down can begin. But we do not have a lot of time. We should start now.

iii) The Vision We Share

'Where there is no vision the people perish' (Prov 29.18, AV). Armed with this text churches which seek to grow will set about forming and presenting a vision into which they can grow. Such vision-forming is important but there are dangers. In our age we deal with a greater diversity of belief and experience than ever before. It is easy for vision statements, if they are carelessly formed or too narrowly conceived, to exclude those who are on a pilgrimage to God. Consider the following (fictitious) vision statement. 'To establish God's kingdom by seeking the conversion of souls to Christ.' A sound statement it may be, but alienating to a postmodern seeker at several points in its terminology (see if you can spot them). How could such a vision statement be restated to give a positive encouragement to that postmodern seeker without compromising the content? Over to you!

The other thing about vision-forming is that it can soon demand suitably qualified people to make the vision work. Damaged or confused people can find themselves excluded here as everywhere else. Vision there must be; but let that vision be of the warm, open, accepting heart of God who takes us as we are and helps us to become what he wants us to be.

Renewal

The gospel we share is also about renewal. It is a pity that the integrity of this great New Testament term has been compromised. I use it here not as a shorthand for a certain kind of church tradition or theological understanding of the Spirit, but as I think the New Testament intended it—that is, to describe the process of being made new in the risen life of Christ. We saw earlier how the processes of the mind can and do atrophy in the face of trends in leisure, work and even education. Paul exhorts people, 'by the mercies of Christ, to be renewed in the spirit of your minds' (Rom 12.2 and Eph 4.23). By that he does not mean the elevation of the intellectual or a return to rationalism. Rather he means a recognition of the richness of a mind appreciative of God and the mystery of his creation, regardless of education, class or race. This richness of a mind in touch with Christ is the reality after which the postmodern gurus, with their emphasis on intuition and emotion, are groping. The promise of the Holy Spirit, integral to our evangelism, is the promise that at every level of our being we can know and be known by God. Our gospel message has to be one which, in presentation and content, speaks of this wholeness.

Then there is a renewal of life. For many the old categories of moral and ethical instruction have become irrelevant. They are compromised because they speak of repression, denial and certain kinds of dominance. The exhortations not to take drugs, not to be promiscuous, not to seek pleasure for its own sake, sound like another way of saying 'do not have a good time.' This is especially the case since they have become divorced from their Christian context. Those who say 'why shouldn't we?' seem to receive the answer 'because I say so.' The implications behind that for many are 'I do not want you to have what I am free to enjoy' and 'I want to be able to remain in control of what you can and cannot do.' The tragedy is that relativism in morals has not brought the release it was expected to deliver. At the same time postmodernism is establishing new absolutes, just as repressive and restrictive as the old ones. 'You cannot say anything is exclusively right or wrong.' 'You must accept all contributions to the debate as being of equal weight.' 'You shall not say anything is unsuitable for television viewing.' So where is freedom? Where is life? Our gospel says; 'For freedom Christ has set you free' (Gal 5.1). It talks about 'dying to our old nature in order to find the new life of Christ' (Rom 6.2). We should believe, understand and share that good news.

And renewal has to mean renewal in worship. That is important for evangelism if the approach I have been advocating is valid.[18] Paul expected that people would see authentic Christian worship and meet God—and that was in Corinth where the church was far from perfect! The hard part is trying to discern what renewal in worship means in practice. I suggest it has less to do with form (and even content) than we sometimes think, and more to do with focus. If we try to develop a certain image or identity through our services simply because we think it will appeal, then we cheat people of the reality for which they search. And if we try to give the service we think the patrons expect and want, we lose the depth of true encounter with God. Renewal in worship has to mean the use of gifts, natural and more immediately God-given, in a way which shows the reality of his presence and the worth of all his people. It has to mean offering the best that we can, in response to his goodness. Visual as well as aural input is important. Flexibility and openness to his leading is more important than tight timing and the performance of a liturgy. Framework there must be, but framework with freedom is better! If we start by contemplating him and let our worship be a response to his beauty and goodness then there will be an integrity and the power of God's presence about what we do. Worship like this leads to integrated lifestyle. By that I mean a lifestyle which reflects and relates to our belief. It is not adequate to worship a God who cares for the poor, loves the brokenhearted and rescues the lost whilst living a life which is self-centred, hard and indifferent. And that is good news indeed to those who only know disruption with themselves, in their relationships, and with God.

Truth-as-Life

Our contemporary society helps us to see two things. One is that truth matters. As Christians we have to state the importance of the concept of truth. We have to do that in the face of clever and persuasive teachers who say there is no truth. The other is that we cannot simply turn the clock back to a former understanding of truth. Unyielding adoption of stated positions is now manifested in

18 J Drane, *Evangelism For a New Age* (Marshall Pickering, 1994) pp 115ff.

all kinds of ugly fundamentalism. Our faith is unique and we should not allow it to be identified with these positions. So how do we proclaim the truth as a new dynamic for the world?

It is in the teaching of Jesus set before us in John's gospel that we find the clue. It is no accident, since John wrote primarily for evangelistic purposes, and arguably into a situation with remarkable similarities to our own. In chapter 8.31-36 we have a powerful presentation of the gospel. Verse 32 states 'You will know the truth and the truth will set you free.' Verse 36 gives a parallel expression, only this time the word 'truth' is replaced by 'Son.' And there is the key. Put this alongside chapter 14.6 and we have the dramatic, beautiful, astonishing claim that truth is; that it is no abstract, dominating, restrictive concept; but is given in personal, loving form, in Jesus himself.

Furthermore, to receive this truth is to be set free. Jesus makes the dramatic claim that to reject him as truth does not result in greater freedom and autonomy. On the contrary. He talks of a slavery—to sin. It is ironic that as a new age discovers the presence and complexity of a world of spiritual forces the poor churchmouse still reels from the attacks of rationalism and hardly dares talk of spiritual warfare.

For many Christian leaders the activity of the forces of darkness is relegated to myth or imagination. But such activity is often experienced by those outside the church in a powerful way, sometimes as a consequence of a way of life which has led people far away from God. In such instances the idea of the gospel giving freedom can be a powerful truth indeed. In a wider sphere we need to recognize with St Paul that there are principalities and powers driving the ideologies and thought patterns which govern people (Eph 6.12). This is why they are not as free as they think they are. But to recognize these dynamics, as Jesus does, is a way back to where we can talk with meaning about the power of truth. Following Jesus—and not just his precepts—is the way to life-as-truth. 'A son belongs to (the family) for ever. So if the Son sets you free, you will be free indeed.' Life in the family of God, through Jesus the Truth, is true freedom for the people around us, and a way ahead for the times in which we live.

5
'Onward and Upward'

Where do we go from here? We do not know what tomorrow's world will be like. There may be reaction against postmodern insights; there may be more complex developments; there may be a combining of the strands we have looked at with new totalitarian trends. But we do know that whatever happens we have the task of sharing the gospel as our duty and our joy. Paul said to the Corinthians; 'Faith, hope and love remain. And the greatest of these is love' (1 Cor 13.13).

Faith

In spite of the recurrent failures of the church and our current sense of being on the margin, God has given a gospel which is sufficient for the needs of this age and the next. Misunderstanding and mishandling does not rob it of its power. Confidence rather than triumphalism—in the gospel rather than in ourselves— can bring us back in touch with the life-wish of Jesus for the world. And our faith in God will help us even to share the parts of the Good News which might not seem good news at the time. There are deeper needs and sensitivities in the world which we may not see but which God's whole truth is designed to meet.

Hope

In a complex, confused situation God is still present. When Ezekiel sat by the waters of Babylon his vision was of God coming out of the north (Ez 1.4). This is not, I regret to say, final proof that God is a Yorkshireman. But it showed Ezekiel that God had been to the traditional stamping-ground of the Babylonian gods and had come away victorious. Whatever principalities and powers preside over today's spiritual confusion, they are not beyond God. Looking to him we can begin to be pro-active in the forming of opinion and value, not simply defensive and reactive in the face of what we meet.

Love

'The greatest of these is love.' Jesus wept in love for a city which had lost its old, traditional standards and was searching for replacements. Love for God and the community burst upon the first century world with dramatic effect. We are assured that love retains its transforming power as the new millennium approaches. But love does not mean paternalistic handouts of 'the truth,' or rapid, patronizing soup-runs into the cultural alleyways before returning, thankfully, to base. It means listening with care; developing a deep knowledge of the questions being asked and the people asking them; seeking real meeting with people and not mere meetings. It means a sense of enjoyment and affection around the positive aspects of our culture, and a genuine sense of mourning for what is destructive. It means entering into and living in the love of God which seeks the greatest good of those he has created in his own image. It means commitment, cost, openness and the joy of realizing our full humanity.

So what does such commitment to love mean for us? It has been said often that we need to be a missionary-based church not a maintenance-based one. What does that mean in practice as we face a new millennium with whatever challenges it might bring? How do we bear and share good news for a postmodern world? Let me tell you what happened to me recently. I was visiting an acquaintance who is a 'new age' kind of person. As we talked he welcomed a visitor to his home. The newcomer, a young student in his early twenties, had hardly sat down before he said. 'Ben. I want to ask you something. How can I learn about personal development, spirituality and meditation? I need to get my head right.' In no time my host had recommended a book on Zen. The episode left me asking several questions. How many ministers, or other Christians come to that, will expect people to come to them so eager and open about their spiritual needs? Why did it happen in this instance? What did Ben have about him which made this possible? (It is not uncommon for people to come to him like this.) The answers may help us forward.

First, his lifestyle is a clear reflection of his beliefs. People know where he stands by the life he lives. Our witness needs to be consistent, and we need to do more serious thinking and obeying in the lives we lead. Do people actually see anything different about the people of God? Until they do they will assume that all they have heard about the shallowness and hypocrisy of the church still stands.

Second, his care is evident to all. He gives people time, courtesy and understanding. He does not assume he has the answer before he has heard the question. Somehow we need to free ourselves from the choke of church activities so that we can be free to listen, learn and love. We also need to have a deep and living interest in the gospel, fed by the love of Christ, so that our witness is a natural outworking of our love for him and for others, not an obligation we feel we must discharge.

Third, when the time came for answers, he knew what to say. If we are going to be ready to give a reason for the hope that is in us then we need quality teaching, active learning, and careful application of our faith. Maybe it is time that our theological colleges and Bible schools made themselves more available to the general Christian public. Short readily accessible courses in faith and communication could be invaluable in helping people know their faith. The questions and experience such people would bring to the courses would help staff make their ministerial training more useful and relevant to today's and tomorrow's needs.

Where are the churches and individual Christians who are making an impact on postmodern society? Perhaps their leaders could share collective insights from their experience. And to undergird the work of effective gospel communication those involved in evangelism could network so as to develop a viable apologetic.

But the last word has to be—spirituality. Closeness to God, openness to his resources, a feeling of his heart for the world will drive us out to live and share the new life of Jesus—good news indeed for a postmodern world.